The Mystery Seed

Maria Valdez
Illustrated by Pat Reynolds

Lenny liked to watch the birds
on the balcony of his apartment.
One day a bird dropped
something from its beak
and flew away.

"I wonder what it is," said Mom.

"It's a seed," said Lenny.
"I'm going to plant it
and see if it grows."

"Good idea!" said Mom.

Lenny planted the seed
in a pot of soil.

Lenny put the pot in the sunshine.
He watered the seed every day.

"I hope the seed sprouts soon,"
he said.

Two weeks later, Lenny saw
a little green shoot.
"Look, Mom, my seed
has sprouted," he said.

"Soon we'll know what your mystery plant is," said Mom.

The green shoot grew into
a tall stem. There were leaves
growing on the stem.

Lenny and his mom moved the plant to a bigger pot. They were careful not to damage its roots.

Then, one day, Lenny saw a bud on his plant. It was facing the sun!

Lenny said, "I think I know
what my mystery plant is!"

Soon the bud opened.

"I was right! It's a sunflower!"

said Lenny.

"It's beautiful," said Mom.
"And soon you can get seeds
from it."

One month later, the sunflower
started to droop.
"Soon we can get the seeds!"
said Lenny.

A week later, Mom helped Lenny
cut the flower. Then they hung it
upside down to dry.

The sunflower seeds started
to drop out.

After the sunflower seeds
dropped out, Lenny and his mom
roasted some of them.

"These taste good!" said Lenny.

"We can feed some seeds
to the birds!" said Lenny.

Lenny and his mom watched
the birds eat the seeds.

"What will you do with the rest
of your seeds?" asked Mom.

"I'll keep these seeds to plant
next spring!" said Lenny.

"Good idea!" said Mom.